A Mother's Book of Prayers

CLASSICS

Written by Julie Mitchell Marra
Illustrated by Hector Garrido

The Regina Press
New York

In memory of my grandmothers,
Mary Mitchell and Marjorie Hessels.

ISBN: 0882716484
Printed in Hong Kong

Table of Contents

Introduction

The prayers in this book were inspired by my mother, my grandmothers and the many friends who have shared their joy of motherhood with me. Whether young or old, every mother shares common concerns and prays for God's protection on her child and her family. From praying to conceive to finding out about a serious illness, mothers are faced with life's experiences of joy and despair. Whatever we are going through, we must remember that God is there with us. We must take some quiet time to pray for his direction.

As I worked with so many loved ones and friends to understand a mother's emotions and experiences, God answered my prayer to become a mother!

I look forward to what lies ahead, and I hope that the simple prayers included in this book will help you, as you face the challenges in your life. You can expand upon these thoughts to make each prayer more specific to your situation.

Whether single, married or widowed, you will find a commonality of fears and hopes that you'll be praying for throughout the many stages of motherhood. And you can know that many mothers will be praying with you.

May this book be a resource for you as you seek God's direction and give him thanks for your family's blessings.

Julie Mitchell Marra

Prayers for all Occasions

Hector Garrido. *Madonna of the Rock,* (Contemporary)

Prayer to Conceive a Child

Dear God,

I am so excited — I'm ready for a baby.

I've dreamed and prayed about this.

Thank You for giving me all that I have.

I pray You will bless me with a baby

in Your time, according to Your will.

I pray for a healthy body to conceive a baby;

for the wisdom to do the right thing;

for patience that it will happen.

Prayer with My Husband

I pray that my husband and I

will understand each other's wishes and needs;

for my body to be in perfect health to conceive.

Show us how to be patient,

always loving each other.

Thank You for giving all of Your children

the greatest gift...life!

Hector Garrido. *The Incarnation,* (Contemporary)

Expecting a Child

What an amazing gift You have given me!
I pray for wisdom to do all the right things to take
care of this precious child inside me;
discernment of what to eat,
how to exercise and how to help this creation of
Yours grow inside of me.
This is truly a miracle!
Thank You!

Thanksgiving for Conception

Dear God,
Thank You for Your greatest gift of life,
for giving me the answer to my prayers,
for blessing me with a child.
This is a dream come true
and I thank You.
I feel like a beautiful rainbow of love
has just appeared in my life.
I look forward to all that
is to come.

Prayer for Mother with Child

Little Baby, I love having you inside me
growing, moving, feeding.
I am eager to see you, but I also love being
pregnant. I pray that we'll always feel this close.
You are God's gift of love to me
and I will always protect, cherish and love you.

Preparing for Baby

I thank You, God, for the love and prayers
of friends and family,
for the home we will provide our baby,
for the bottles and booties and bassinets.
I rejoice in all the blessings I have received.

For a Happy, Healthy Baby

Lord in heaven,
Send my little baby Your blessings,
Fill my baby with peace and happiness,
Keep this child under protection.

Prayer for Single Mothers

Lord, You are my guiding Shepherd,
You are all I need.
I trust You to give me knowledge and strength
to be the best parent to my little one.
I pray that I will show my child
Your love and understanding
in all I do and say.
I know it won't always be easy,
but I do know You'll always be there.

Miscarriage

Dear God,
I can't understand why this happened.
I know You have a plan for everything,
but I didn't think I'd lose my precious little baby.
Help me not to be angry.
I'm upset and my emotions are taking control.
I feel lonely, cold and unhappy.
Lead me to Your side,
Your warmth and Your joy.

Infertility

I know You have a plan for each of us.
I prayed that Your plan for me
would include having children.
Sometimes I have difficulty understanding
why I can't conceive.
Grant me Your wisdom to come to terms
with not having my own children.
Open my mind and heart
and prepare me
to love another child who needs me.

Looking to Adopt

Please help me to adopt a child.
So many mothers can't keep their babies,
and I am unable to have one.
Lead me to the right people
and, ultimately, the baby who needs me.
Grant me patience
until I find a little one to adopt.

Prayer for Adopted Baby

God,
Thank You for leading me to this child,
perfect in every way.
I never dreamed that I could love so much.
Give me the insight
to handle questions and situations
that may arise in our family,
neighborhood and school.
Help me to be the best mother I can be.

For a Happy, Easy Delivery

Dear God,
You have asked me to carry and deliver this baby
safely into the world.
Please let the delivery of this child go smoothly
and without complications.
I know that You will be watching over me
and my precious little child.
We've waited a long time for this child.
We pray for Your blessings during this labor of love

Boy or Girl?

God, You have blessed us with a baby.
Whether it's a boy or a girl, we will love it dearly.
Please help us accept Your choice
and not feel disappointed.
Show us the beauty of all Your creations.

For My Doctor

Dear Lord,
Bless my doctor with strength and patience
should my labor last a long time.
Please give my doctor wisdom and skill
to help You bring this baby into the world.

When Baby Is Born

Lord, You have performed another miracle.
You are the giver of life,
and I give You all the glory
for this little miracle of life named (name).
I pray for Your angels to watch over my child.

For Newborn

Dear Lord,
You blessed me with
a precious baby.
I'm so happy.
Please show me Your way
to bring up this child.
Help me to love this little one
as You love us.

Loss of Newborn

Dear God,
Only You know Your purpose for this.
You have taken my child to heaven.
I can still feel my baby's warm body
and hear my baby's cry.
I know my baby is with You.
But I can't stop mourning,
and I wish my baby were here with me.
Help me through my grief.

Hector Garrido. *Madonna of the Night,* (Contempora

Nursing/Feeding

As my little baby takes nourishment
I thank You for providing for us.
This child is so small
and depends on me for everything.
You have blessed me with all I need.
I pray my baby will grow strong from this milk
and will find nourishment for its body and soul.

Changing Diapers

Everything I do for my baby I do with thanks to You.
May I be able to take care of my little baby,
filling every need,
just as You have taken care of me.

Cranky Baby

Sometimes my baby cries for hours.
I would do anything to make my child happy.
Please help me to be patient when I feel discouraged.
I'm frustrated because I can't relieve
the discomfort my child must be feeling.

William Luberoff. *Adoring Madonna, (Contemporary)*

My Baby Is Not Sleeping

Lord,
I'm so tired that I feel delirious.
Please watch over me.
I know that accidents can happen when
I'm sleepy and not thinking clearly.
I pray my baby and I will soon be able to sleep.
Thank You for Your gift of rest.

Nighttime Blessings

Lord,
Bless our family this evening.
There is so much sin and sickness in the world;
tonight we ask for Your everlasting strength
to overcome all that is wrong.
We know we can find
peace and shelter in You,
following Your Word every day.
Thank You for this day.
I pray for a restful, peaceful sleep.
Good night, Lord.

Overwhelmed Times

Feeding the baby,
cleaning the house,
doing the laundry,
the shopping,
the list goes on and on.
And that's all before and after
 I put in a full day at work.
Dear Lord, give me energy
and time to get everything done.

When I Go to Work

I never realized what "having it all" meant.
Now, sometimes it feels like "too much."
Thank You for my job that helps
provide for my family.
I know I'm blessed, and others have so much less.
I pray for the energy to be a mother and to work.
I pray for my baby to stay healthy and safe.
I pray for my supervisor to be patient and
understanding when my baby needs me.

Time Management

I used to feel in control of my day.
Now there are so many things to get done.
I'm feeling discouraged and overloaded.
I know You are ultimately in control.
I pray You'll lead me
to accomplish what is necessary
and not to get anxious about
what doesn't get done.

Husband's Concerns

Dear Lord, My husband is worried about
the baby and the money we'll need
for our family's necessities.
He seems distant.
Maybe it's because I give so much
attention to the baby.
Please help him realize that You will provide
and that You will bless us as we follow You.
I pray for Your direction in my relationship with him.
Help me to give him the love he needs from me.

When Baby Is Sick

Lord,
I feel so helpless.
My baby's sick and neither of us have slept all night.
Help me to stay alert
and attentive to my baby's needs.
Help the doctor to give us a method of recovery.
I pray for Your healing power.

When Baby Cries

Our baby cries nonstop, all night long.
We can't get any sleep.
It seems that's all I hear.
My husband leaves for work without rest.
This situation is making us unhappy and tense.
It makes me want to cry, too!
Please help us to find joy in our lives again.

Daycare

In today's world, I have chosen to work,
and I'm trying to be financially responsible.
But sometimes when I drop off my child
I feel irresponsible.
Please help me not to worry!
"What if someone harms my child?"
"What if they neglect my baby's needs?"
"What damage am I doing to my child?"
Dear Lord, please send Your angels
to watch over my little one.
Help me to trust.

Poor Health

I know, Lord, my child has a serious illness.
Help me to make my baby comfortable.
If I could take this sickness from my baby,
I would gladly bear it.
I know You have a plan for all of us.
Please show me how to care for my child.

Mental Retardation

Every child is a gift from You, I know.
Help me to understand
this dear child.
I can't stop asking, "Why?"
I pray You'll give me the wisdom to
raise our child in love and grace,
to help my child have the best life possible.
Please protect my child
from danger
and harmful words.

Living with a Handicap

I am reminded that no human is perfect.
I pray that You will use me to reveal
that same message to my child.
Help my little one to overcome this handicap
and realize Your love is for everyone.

Getting to Nursery School

It's usually hectic
getting my family out in the morning.
When my child leaves for nursery school,
I'm not only stressed,
but I am nervous and worried.
Will my child get into trouble,
be in danger, get hurt?"
I fear not knowing what will happen.
Please give me the peace
to let go and leave You in charge.

When Accidents Happen

My heart felt like it stopped when I heard that crash.
And I ran to see my little one red-faced and crying.
I was scared and then angry.
Please help me to show my child
that we are not perfect
and that accidents happen to everyone.
Help me to teach my child
to avoid accidents in the future.

Being a Single Working Parent

God,
I feel so alone.
Some days seem so stressful!
Getting my little one off to school,
and me to work on time.
Sometimes I have to leave work
to take care of my child.
Please help my supervisor understand.
Please help me to meet all of my obligations.

For Safety at School

I hear about accidents and violence
on school buses and in schools.
As I send my little one on this school bus,
I pray for Your guardian angels
to protect and keep my child safe.
Grant wisdom to all adults
who are responsible for children —
bus drivers, teachers and caregivers.

Hector Garrido. *Madonna and Child,* (Contemporar

Curiosity

Dear God,
May Your angels follow my little one
who seems to be getting into everything,
eating everything and throwing everything.
I know this is a stage of development — curiosity
Give me patience to be free from anxiety
while keeping my child safe.

Doing Chores

Dear God,
Some days it feels
overwhelming.
Dishes, laundry, feeding, bathing, work,
and then everyone wants a loving smile from me.
I'm exhausted.
There's no such thing as rest time or sleep.
I'm not sure I can keep up.
I know You are my rock and my fortress.
In You, I find strength.
Thank You for helping me get through today.

Philippe De Champaigne. *The Nativity.* (1602-167

For My Child's Future

God,
I pray that my child will have the resources
for a successful future.
Please continue to watch over
my child as You have in the past.
Thank You for not asking me
to be a perfect parent;
I will try to be the best parent I can.

For a Sibling of a New Baby

I am sensing that my child is not happy.
It's been going on since
I brought the new baby home.
I think my child resents the attention
we give the new baby.
Help me to show my child how much love I have.
That love is multiplied through You.

Going on Vacation

I pray for Your protection on this vacation.
Keep our home safe while we're away.
Watch over our family
and help us to grow from this experience.
There's so much about Your world
for us to learn and discover!

On a Child's Accomplishments

What a blessing!
My little one has achieved so much,
and I give You the glory!
When I look into my child's eyes
I thank You that through me
You created this wonderful little human being.
It's truly amazing.
Thank You, God.

Hector Garrido. *Bethlehem,* (Contemporary)

For a Caregiver
Dear Lord,
I trust this caregiver
with my child.
If an emergency arises,
please give our care-giver the instincts
to do what it takes to keep my child safe.

For Teachers and Mentors of My Child
Lord, let the teachers and mentors
in my child's life
be strong in faith
and solid in purpose.
My child looks to others
to learn about life.
I see You working in their lives and in my child's.
Please direct them according to Your will.
Help us all work together for Your good
and according to Your purpose.

For Fidelity

Dear God,
The love You made for the two of us
is still there;
it's a bond that will never break.
You keep it strong.
I pray
that we will both always gain strength from You
and nurture that love we first felt for each other.
As life becomes routine,
may we never break the vows we made.

For Guidance

Help us as parents
to understand our children's needs,
their strengths and their weaknesses.
We know we don't have all the answers,
but we will look to You for guidance.

Setting an Example

Lord,
You have set an example for all of us.
Please make us strong and shining examples
so that our children will not doubt
what is wrong or right.
Fill us with Your wisdom, strength and courage
to do what is right.

My Husband Has an Addiction

Lord,
Please help my husband to face his addiction
and to find the strength to overcome it.
I pray that he will come to me
for the help he needs
and that I will have the wisdom to help him.
Lord, lead him to recovery.

Overcoming My Addiction

Dear God,

I am sorry.

I am addicted, and I'm not sure how to stop.

Help me to overcome this addiction.

I will focus on just this one day.

Thank You for Your forgiveness.

When My Husband is Overworked

My husband came in so late
that he didn't even see the baby.
Instead of understanding
that he'd had a rough day,
I questioned why he was late.
Please help me to be more understanding.
I don't like to argue, and when I start
interrogating him, that's what we end up doing.
Give him the strength to stay healthy
during such demanding days.
And help me to be patient.
I know he's just trying to give our family
the best he can.

When My Husband Travels

When my husband travels
I wonder what interesting people he's meeting
and what exciting things he's doing.
And then I wonder when he gets home to me,
and things are not as exciting...will he be happy?
Or will he want to go away again?
Lord, keep me from feeling insecure.
I pray for my husband's safe journey
and that he will keep our family
in his heart and mind always.

Priorities

Money, Cars, Home, Stocks, Education,
Family, Jobs, Church, Sunday School, Retirement
our priorities are confusing and all mixed up.
We need to sit down
and talk about where we are
and where we are going.
Help us find that time
and help us to be realistic
and honest with each other.

Sandro Boticelli. *Madonna and Child (Detail)*, (1445-15

Angry at Each Other

Our argument was loud
and I said a lot of things I didn't mean.
But he was also wrong about a few things.
Help me to say I'm sorry and accept his apology.
Help us learn to resolve conflicts
without verbal violence
and to strengthen our relationship.
My biggest fear is that my children will hear
and be afraid or think that is the way to act
toward someone you love.
Please help us set a good example
of loving relationships.

Angry at My Child

Dear God, I wish I could just get inside my child's head
to know what my child is thinking.
Please give me patience and understanding
and strength.
Grant me the wisdom
and the courage to let my child grow up
to be the person my child wants to be.

Money Pressures

We're living paycheck to paycheck.
There's debt we owe and yet there are things we need.
Help us work through these tight days,
knowing we have more than so many others
and that You have always provided for us.

Loss of Husband's Job

We were struggling to make ends meet
and now my husband lost his job.
He's depressed and down and I'm upset and anxious.
Dear Lord, please lead my husband to a good job
and help our family live within our means.

Loss of My Job

Lord, I need Your help.
I've lost my job and I can't handle this loss in income.
I pray this loss will lead me to a new
and better job very soon.
Help me to have the courage and wisdom
to seek new opportunities.
Give me patience to wait for the right job for me.

Divorce

I know it's not Your plan
for us to get divorced.
I have tried to save this relationship,
but we've gone our separate ways
and my heart is breaking.
Help me to live without him.
I pray that both of us will always
communicate with our children
and that we can both help them understand
that there's no blame
or anger directed at them.

Infidelity

Here I am, wife, mother, partner, friend.
Betrayed.
What do I do now, Lord? What are my choices?
Break up the family?
Forgive and forget?
Please help me to make the right decisions
for me, for my children and for You.

Being a Divorced Mother

Problems seem to arise whenever
my child's father gets involved.
Help me to open my heart to him
so that my child can know his father.
I know how important a father's love is.
Help me to have the wisdom and
the energy to raise this child alone,
yet share the child's love with another.

Temptations

So often I am tempted by the world's influences.
Help me to have the willpower and the strength
to do what is right for me and my family.

Correcting My Child

Please give me the knowledge
to correct my child wisely and lovingly.
Stop me from being unreasonable or overly angry.
Give me the grace in my tired times
to show motherly love in my discipline.

For My Teen to Follow the Example of Jesus

I know this is a difficult time
in my child's life.
Help my child to look to Jesus.
Give my child the courage
to stand up to peer pressure.
Grant my teenager the discernment
to know the right thing to do.
In every situation, help my child
to understand what Jesus would do.

Child's First Date

God,
My child is on a first date
and I'm worried.
Help me to remain calm
knowing I have raised my child to understand
the difference between wrong and right.
I trust my child will do the right thing.
Keep these two young people in Your care.
May their time together be sweet and safe.

For Restraint

When we're young,
it seems as though nothing
can touch us or harm us.
When we are young,
sexual attraction is new and exciting.
I know.
I lived through it too.
Now I pray that the values
we instilled in our children
will protect them.

For Teens Facing Temptation

Dear God,
Please protect my child.
Give my child wisdom and discernment.
Being a teen today is fast, fun and easy.
Show me how to open my child's eyes to
how today's actions can affect their future.
I pray for the Holy Spirit to help my child
resist peer pressure and temptation.

Finding Out About Drug Use

God,
I pray for my child's safety.
Help this young person find
the resources and assistance
to change direction
and walk in Your way.
Help me to be strong and loving.
And lead us to recovery.

For Good Mentors

There are stories of mentors
who have abused their power
and taken advantage of children.
I hear of some
who don't even like children.
Please guide my child
to those who are honest and good and true.

Materialism

Dear God,
The world puts such an emphasis
on the things that money can buy.
My child complains about not having enough.
Help my teen understand
that material possessions are temporary
and do not lead to happiness.

Working Mother

My child is busy with school and other activities.
I am busy working.
We don't spend much time together.
We don't talk much.
Please protect my soon-to-be-adult child
and help me know when I am really needed.
Help my supervisor understand
my need to be available for my child.

First Job
Sometimes I wish that my child
wouldn't have to work.
It's so much to balance —
work, school, friends,
homework, dances and family.
Help my child grow
in responsibility and maturity.

Sex
I just found out my child is having sex.
Give me the courage
to talk to my child about the seriousness of this.
Give me wisdom and strength
to guide my child in the right direction.
I pray that I will always
keep the lines of communication open
to help my child become a responsible young adult

Wayward Child

I can't believe my child has left.
Gone out to a world of violence and danger.
I walk around the house waiting.
At night, I dream that my child is home again,
only to wake with a loneliness in my heart
and fear in my stomach.
Please inspire my child to contact me.
I pray that I can let my young adult leave,
yet keep the door to my home open.

For Driving

There are so many crazy drivers out there.
I pray my child will be a defensive driver.
Please help my child to resist the temptation
to speed,
to run red lights,
to tailgate,
and to drive recklessly.
And help me, Lord, to be calm,
to trust my teen with the responsibility,
knowing Your angels are watching.

or Graduation

m so proud of my child...
t I've lost my baby.
ive me the courage to let go.
know there are big obstacles and pitfalls ahead,
t I pray that my child makes it through each one
th a lesson learned.
ay my child continue
owing up the ladder of success.

ingle Parent Loneliness

y child's room is empty.
wait for laughter and music to fill it once again.
lease guide me in this next step of my life.
elp me to find something to fill the void.
elp me not make my child
el guilt or blame for my loneliness.
t my child visit because my child wants to.

Death of a Child

How can a mother outlive her child?
My world is frozen, I'm trying to talk but I can't
More than ever I need Your love to fill my heart
so I won't become angry or resentful.
Help me live without my child
and find some peace in my time
knowing that in Your time
You'll bring us together again.

While Stressed

Some days just start out and finish WRONG.
Everyone has a problem
and expects me to drop what I'm doing,
while I'm trying to work through
some problems of my own.
Help me through these days without
keeping it all inside until I explode!
Just talking to You helps me unwind.
Thank You.

Caravaggio. *The Burial of Jesus*, (1571-16

During Difficult Days

I feel like the years have just flown by
and I'm getting older.
My life is changing...family...work...friends...
things are different.
I know You send each of us on our own cycle of
life.
Help me to make
smooth transitions
Knowing You have blessings
for me in the future.

Child Getting Married

Only yesterday
I held this child in my arms.
Today my child is starting a whole new life.
May it be filled with joy
and may it be fulfilling.
I pray they will open their hearts to You,
knowing You are present in their marriage.

On Being a Grandparent

Oh, thank You, God,
for this blessing.
I pray that I will be a good grandmother —
one who shows my grandchildren
how special they are
and teaches them about
their heritage.
Give me the wisdom to know
when to give advice and
when to give my children freedom
to raise their children in their own way.

When Child Leaves Home

Oh, God,
it hurts to have my child move away.
I know my child is Your child always, too.
I ask that You always watch over my child.

When Angry

Why am I angry?
How can I be so selfish?
Lord, I try to be like You
but I am human,
and I'm mad right now.
I know it's not right for me to be angry...
I ask You to fill my heart and mind with Your lov
With Your help, I know I can show love not ang
even when something or someone
still doesn't make sense to me.

Homosexual Child

Lord,
You know that
I will always love and help my child
through whatever difficulties lie ahead.
Please help me overcome my fears.
Help us keep our relationship strong.
Please guide and protect this child
in Your safe and loving ways.

Death of My Husband

was not something I thought would happen.
We all have those romantic ideas of dying
in old age with our mate.
What do I do now, God?
You've taken my husband.
Whom I relied on, depended on.
Is not something I can easily accept.
In fact, I'd like to go to sleep
and wake up again with everything like it was.
Please give me the strength I need right now
to keep my faith in Your everlasting promise
that we will be together again.

Mid-life Prayer

Wasn't it just yesterday that I had children in diapers?
Suddenly I'm middle aged.
Help me enjoy this ride and live every day to its fullest.
Prepare me for the twists and turns that lie ahead.
Help me accept what is to come
and look forward to the future.

Loneliness

Today I'm feeling old and unwanted.
It seems like no one wants to be bothered
to come visit or call.
There's nothing to do, my housework is done,
I have no new books,
I keep the television on for company.
I would call my family, but they have their own live
They are always busy.
I know they love me and visit when they can.
Help me find joy in Your presence and peace in
this quiet time before I see my family again.

Do I Have Enough Money?

Things are a little tight now.
What about my future?
I know You will provide for me.
Help me trust that my needs will be met.
I pray for Your calm love
to fill my heart so that I will not worry,
but believe in Your promises of blessings.

Sassoferrato. *Our Lady of Sorrows,* (1605-1(

Simplifying Life and Enjoying Freedom

I don't know if this big house is necessary for me
It's nice to have a place for my children
to stay when they visit but it's overwhelming now
— housework, expense.
I don't want lots of things.
I want to see places I haven't seen.
I want to make my life simpler.
I want to make it easier to get up and
go when I can. Lead me, Lord.

Priorities

Dear Lord, a long time ago
it seemed that all my focus was on my children.
I can barely remember
when I thought about me.
Now my life has changed
and it's time to prioritize.
Please help me do what is right for me
and let my children know
I've not forgotten them.

In Menopause

People think I'm crazy.
I'm hot, I'm moody, I don't know what
I'll be like any time of the day.
My family tries to be supportive,
but I know it's difficult to understand
unless you've been through it.
Help me through this time.
Give me the strength to overcome.

Finding Out about Serious Illness

This news about my husband's illness
has really stunned me.
I'm trying to do the best for him, but
every time I think about it or look at him,
my eyes well up with tears.
I feel so hopeless and alone.
I know that only You know the time
we will be called to You.
But please, I pray that You will heal my husband
and give me the strength to do
everything I can to help him.

Coming to Terms with Mortality

I know You created us for life here on earth
and that through You
we will receive eternal life in heaven.
But I'm not sure how I feel about dying.
Now I have been told I have a serious illness.
God, grant me understanding so I can bravely fac
each day and relish every minute of all my days.
Thank You for all I have been given in this life.
Help me look forward to what is to come.

Loss of My Husband

Never could I have imagined living without him.
I'm trying to be strong for my family,
but I feel like I'm play-acting.
I'm trying to play a part,
but I'm not feeling like me.
The real me wants to scream and cry and lock
myself in my room, until I get him back.
Will You please help me
heal the heaviness I have on my heart?
Grant me Your peace.

Loss of a Friend

I've lost my friend.
How will I share my good and bad news of the day?
I will miss my friend terribly.
Please help me find Your companionship
during this time of loss.
I pray for Your gracious blessing upon my friend.
I hope Your gift of eternal salvation awaits my friend.
Please help me find new joy in the days ahead.

Facing Handicaps

I am grateful for my life itself
but sometimes just living is hard!
I don't like being
a burden on others.
I'm afraid they'll think
I'm a nuisance.
Help me to be as independent as I can be,
to have the courage to ask for help
when I need it,
and to accept help with a gracious and loving heart.

Going Home to God

Thank You, God, for this life.
I have had great times and not-so-great times,
but I always learned something from them.
Thank You
for standing by my side and guiding me.
Please forgive my sins and
take care of my loved ones.
Help them understand that I had a good life,
and I am ready to leave it
to be with You.

Hector Garrido. *The Assumption of Mary.* (Contempora

Catholic Prayers and Devotions

The Rosary of the Blessed Virgin Mary

The devotion of the Rosary contributes greatly to the destruction of sin, the recovery of grace, and the promotion of the glory of God. Gregory XVI

The Rosary is the most popular of all the Marian devotions. It was revealed to St. Dominic by the Blessed Mother, and begun in the fifteenth century by Alen de Rupe, a Dominican preacher. The Rosary combines both vocal and meditative prayer, and is treasured by all who use it. The beginnings of the Rosary are found in the early Christian practice of reciting the 150 Psalms from the Bible, either daily or weekly, as a way of prayer. Those unable to recite the Psalms began to recite 150 prayers, mainly the Our Father, 150 times, often using beads to count the prayers. By medieval times the custom of saying Paternoster beads (the Latin for Our Father) was common in many countries of Europe. While saying the prayers it was customary to meditate on the mysteries of the life of Jesus, from his birth to his resurrection. The Rosary its present form arose in late medieval Christianity.

The Hail Mary

The Hail Mary evolved as a prayer from the devotion of medieval men and women who saw Mary, the mother of Jesus, as the great witness to his life, death and resurrection. Its earliest form was the greeting made to Mary by the Angel Gabriel:

> *Hail Mary,*
> *full of grace,*
> *the Lord is with you*   *Luke 1:28*

Over time the greeting given to Mary by her cousin Elizabeth was added:

> *Blessed are you among women*
> *and blessed is the fruit of your womb.* *Luke 1:42*

Finally by the fifteenth century, the remainder of the prayer appeared:

> *Holy Mary, mother of God,*
> *pray for us sinners*
> *now and at the hour of our death.*

he prayer calls upon Mary, full of grace and close to
er Son, to intercede for us sinners now and at the time
ur death. We share her as a mother with St. John to
hom Jesus entrusted her, when on Calvary Jesus said,
ehold your mother. She will always bring Christ into
ur life. We trust her to care for us as she cared for the
wly married couple at Cana in Galilee. We can go to
er in our need.

By the end of the sixteenth century the practice
saying 150 Hail Marys in series or decades of 10 was
opular among many ordinary Christian people. The
ysteries of the life, death and resurrection of Jesus,
ntained in the Joyful, Sorrowful and Glorious
ysteries, were remembered during these prayers.

osa Mystica

The name rosary comes from the flower, the
se, which in medieval times was seen as a symbol of life
ernal. Mary, the first to be redeemed by Christ, has
en called Mystical Rose. She reminds us we are called
the eternal life of Paradise.

How to Say the Rosary

The complete Rosary consists of fifteen decades, but is further divided into three distinct parts, each containing five decades called the Joyful, the Sorrowful, and the Glorious Mysteries. The Mysteries of the Rosary symbolize important events from the lives of both our Lord and the Blessed Mother.

Each decade contains one mystery, an "Our Father," ten "Hail Marys," and a "Glory be to the Father." To say the Rosary, begin by making the sign of the cross and saying "The Apostles' Creed" on the crucifix, one "Our Father" on the first bead, three "Hail Marys" on the next three beads, and then a "Glory be to the Father." When this is finished, meditate upon the first mystery, say an "Our Father," ten "Hail Marys," and one "Glory to the Father." The first decade is now complete, and to finish the Rosary proceed in the same manner until all five decades have been said.

The Five Joyful Mysteries

Mondays and Thursdays

1. **The Annunciation**
   The Angel Gabriel tells Mary that she is to be the Mother of God. *Humility*

2. **The Visitation**
   The Blessed Virgin pays a visit to her cousin Elizabeth. *Charity*

3. **The Nativity**
   The Infant Jesus is born in a stable at Bethlehem. *Poverty*

4. **The Presentation**
   The Blessed Virgin presents the Child Jesus to Simeon in the Temple. *Obedience*

5. **The Finding in the Temple**
   Jesus is lost for three days, and the Blessed Mother finds him in the Temple. *Piety*

The Five Sorrowful Mysteries

Tuesdays and Fridays

1. The Agony in the Garden
Jesus prays in the Garden of Olives and drops of blood break through his skin.

Contrition

2. The Scourging at the Pillar
Jesus is tied to a pillar and cruelly beaten with whips.

Purity

3. The Crowning with Thorns
A crown of thorns is placed upon Jesus' head.

Courage

4. The Carrying of the Cross
Jesus is made to carry his cross to Calvary.

Patience

5. The Crucifixion
Jesus is nailed to the cross, and dies for our sins.

Self-denial

The Five Glorious Mysteries

Wednesdays, Saturdays and Sundays

1. The Resurrection
Jesus rises from the dead, three days after his death. *Fai*

2. The Ascension
Forty days after his death, Jesus ascends into heaven. *Hop*

3. The Descent of the Holy Spirit
Ten days after the Ascension, the Holy Spirit comes to the apostles and the Blesse Mother in the form of fiery tongues. *Lo*

4. The Assumption
The Blessed Virgin dies and is assumed in heaven. *Eternal Happines*

5. The Crowning of the Blessed Virgin
The Blessed Virgin is crowned Queen of Heaven and Earth by Jesus, her Son.

Devotion to Mar

Hail, Holy Queen

Hail, holy Queen, mother of mercy, our life, our sweetness, and our hope.

To you we cry, poor banished children of Eve; to you we send up our sighs, mourning and weeping in this valley of tears.

Turn then, O most gracious advocate, your eyes of mercy toward us, and after this our exile, show unto us the blessed fruit of your womb, Jesus.

O clement, O loving, O sweet Virgin Mary.

V. Pray for us, O holy Mother of God

R. That we may be made worthy of the promises of Christ.

Let us pray.

O God, whose only begotten Son, by his life, death and Resurrection, has purchased for us the rewards of eternal life, grant, we beseech You, that meditating upon these Mysteries of the most Holy Rosary of the Blessed Virgin Mary, we may imitate what they contain and obtain what they promise.

Through the same Christ our Lord. Amen.

PRAYERS TO THE BLESSED VIRGIN MARY

The Hail Mary

Hail Mary, full of grace,
the Lord is with you.
Blessed are you among women,
and blessed is the fruit
of your womb, Jesus.

Holy Mary, Mother of God,
pray for us sinners,
now and at the hour of our death. Amen.

The Memorare

Remember, O most gracious Virgin Mary,
that never was it known that
anyone who fled to your protection,
implored your help,
or sought your intercession
was left unaided.

Inspired by this confidence, we fly unto you,
O Virgin of virgins, our Mother!

To you we come, before you we stand,
sinful and sorrowful.

O Mother of the Word incarnate,
despise not our petitions, but in your mercy
hear and answer us. Amen.

The Magnificat

My soul proclaims the greatness
    of the Lord and my spirit
    exults in God my savior;
    because he has looked upon his
    lowly handmaid.

Yes, from this day forward
    all generations will call me blessed,
    for the Almighty
    has done great things for me.

Holy is his name, and his mercy reaches
    from age to age
    for those who fear him,

He has shown the power of his arm,
    he has routed the proud of heart.

He has pulled down princes
    from their thrones and
    exalted the lowly.

The hungry he has filled with good
    things, the rich sent empty away.

He has come to the help of Israel
    his servant, mindful of his mercy –
    according to the promise he made
    to our ancestors – of his mercy to
    Abraham and to his descendants
    for ever.

The Regina Caeli
"Queen of Heaven"

Queen of heaven, rejoice, Alleluia.
   The Son whom you were privileged to bear,
   Alleluia, has risen as he said, Alleluia.

Pray to God for us, Alleluia.

Rejoice and be glad, Virgin Mary,
   Alleluia.
   For the Lord has truly risen. Alleluia.

Let us pray. O God
   it was by the resurrection of
   your Son,
   our Lord Jesus Christ,
   that you brought joy to the world.

Grant that through the intercession of the
   Virgin Mary, his Mother, we may attain the
   joy of eternal life.

Through Christ, our Lord. Amen.

The Angelus

The angel of the Lord declared unto Mary.

And she conceived of the Holy Spirit. Hail
   Mary...

Behold the handmaid of the Lord.

Be it done to me according to your word. Hail
   Mary...

And the Word was made flesh;
   and dwelt among us. Hail Mary...

Pray for us, O holy Mother of God, that we
   may be made worthy
   of the promises of Christ.

Let us pray.

Pour forth, we beseech You, O Lord, Your
   grace in our hearts, that we, to whom the
   Incarnation of Christ, Your Son, was made
   known
   by the message of an angel,
   may by his passion and cross
   be brought to the glory of his resurrection
   through the same Christ our Lord.
   Amen.

Hector Garrido. *The Annunciation* (Contempora

Litany of the Blessed Virgin Mary

Lord, have mercy,

Christ, have mercy

Lord, have mercy.

Christ, hear us.

Christ, graciously hear us.

God, the Father of heaven, have mercy on us

God, the Son, Redeemer of the world, have
mercy on us.

God, the Holy Spirit, have mercy on us.

Holy Trinity, one God, have mercy on us.

Holy Mary, *(after each invocation, respond
with, "Pray for us")*

Pray for us.

Holy Mother of God,

Holy Virgin of virgins,

Mother of Christ,

Mother, full of grace,

Mother most pure,

Mother most chaste,

Immaculate Mother,

Sinless Mother,

Lovable Mother,

Model of Mothers,

Mother of good counsel,

Mother of our Maker,
Mother of our Savior,
Wisest of virgins,
Holiest of virgins,
Virgin, powerful in the sight of God,
Virgin, merciful to us sinners,
Virgin, faithful to all God asks of you,
Mirror of holiness,
Seat of wisdom,
Cause of our joy,
Shrine of the Spirit,
Honor of your people,
Devoted handmaid of the Lord,
Mystical rose,
Tower of David,
Tower of ivory,
House of gold,
Ark of the covenant,
Gate of heaven,
Star of hope,
Health of the sick,
Refuge of sinners,
Comfort of the afflicted,

Help of Christians,

Queen of angels,

Queen of patriarchs,

Queen of prophets,

Queen of apostles,

Queen of martyrs,

Queen of confessors,

Queen of virgins,

Queen of all saints,

Queen conceived in holiness,

Queen raised up to glory,

Queen of the Rosary,

Queen of peace,

Lamb of God, You take away the sins
of the world, – Spare us, O Lord.

Lamb of God, You take away the sins
of the world, – Graciously hear us, O
Lord.

Lamb of God, You take away the sins
of the world, – Have mercy on us.

Pray for us, O holy Mother of God,
– That we may be made worthy
of the promises of Christ.

Let us pray.

Filippino Lippi. *The Virgin in Adoration* (Detail), (c. 1457-150

Lord God,
  give to Your people the joy of
  continual health in mind and body.

With the prayers of the Virgin Mary
  to help us, guide us through
  the sorrows of this life to
  eternal happiness in the life to come.

We ask this through Christ our Lord.
  Amen.

Prayer to St. Gerard for Motherhood

O glorious St. Gerard,
powerful intercessor before God, and
wonder worker of our day,
I call upon you and seek your help. You
who always fulfilled God's will on earth,
help me to do God's holy will. Intercede
with the Giver of life, from whom all
parenthood proceeds, that I may conceive
and raise children who will please God
in this life, and be heirs to the
kingdom of heaven. Amen.

Family Prayer

God made us a family.
We need one another.
We love one another.
We forgive one another.
We work together.
We play together.
We worship together.
Together we use God's word.
Together we grow in Christ.
Together we love all people.
Together we serve our God.
Together we hope for heaven.
These are our hopes
and ideals.
Help us to attain them,
O God, through Jesus Christ
our Lord.

Prayer for the Helpless Unborn

Heavenly Father, in Your love for
us, protect against the wickedness of the devil,
those helpless little ones to whom You have
given the gift of life.

Touch with pity the hearts of those women
pregnant in our world today who are not
thinking of motherhood.

Help them to see that the child they carry is
made in Your image – as well as theirs – made
for eternal life.

Dispel their fear and selfishness and give them
true womanly hearts to love their babies and give
them birth and all the needed care that
a mother alone can give.

We ask this through Jesus Christ, Your Son, our
Lord, who lives and reigns with You and the
Holy Spirit, one God, forever and ever. Amen.

Filippo Lippi. *The Virgin Mary*, (c. 1406-1469)

Prayer for Safe Delivery

O great St. Gerard, beloved servant of Jesus Christ, perfect imitator of your meek and humble Savior, and devoted child of the Mother of God, enkindle within my heart one spark of that heavenly fire of charity which glowed in your heart and made you an angel of love.

O glorious St. Gerard, because when falsely accused of crime, you did bear, like your Divine Master, without murmur or complaint, the calumnies of wicked men, you have been raised up by God as the patron and protector of expectant mothers.

Preserve me from danger and from the excessive pains accompanying childbirth, and shield the child which I now carry, that it may see the light of day and receive the purifying and life-giving waters of baptism through Jesus Christ our Lord. Amen.

(Nine Hail Marys)

EVERYDAY PRAYERS

ign of the Cross

In the name of the Father,
and of the Son, ✟ and of the
Holy Spirit.
Amen.

he Lord's Prayer

Our Father, who art in heaven,
hallowed be thy name;
thy kingdom come;
thy will be done on earth as it is
in heaven.

Give us this day our daily bread;
and forgive us our trespasses
as we forgive those who trespass against us;
and lead us not into temptation,
but deliver us from evil.
Amen.

Glory Be to the Father

Glory be to the Father, and to the Son, and to the Holy Spirit.

As it was in the beginning, is now and eve shall be, world without end. Amen.

Grace Before Meals

Bless us, O Lord, and these Your gifts which we are about to receive

from your bounty,

through Christ our Lord. Amen.

Grace After Meals

We give You thanks, Almighty God, for these and all Your blessings;

You live and reign for ever and ever. Amen.

Bartolomeo Murillo. *The Holy Family,* (1618-168

Come Holy Spirit

Come, Holy Spirit, fill the hearts
  of Your faithful and
  kindle in them the fire of your love.
Send forth Your Spirit,
  and they shall be created; And You will
  renew the face of the earth.
O God,
  on the first Pentecost
  You instructed the hearts of those who
  believed in you.
  By the light of the Holy Spirit;
  under the inspiration of the same Spirit,
  give us a taste
  for what is right and true
  and a continuing sense
  of his presence and power;
  through Jesus Christ our Lord. Amen.

Hector Garrido. *Kneeling Madonna, (Contemporary*

An Act of Faith

O God,
   I firmly believe all the truths
   that you have revealed
   and that you teach us
   through your Church,
   for you are truth itself and
   can neither deceive nor be deceived.

An Act of Hope

O God,
   I hope with complete trust
   that You will give me,
   through the merits of Jesus Christ, all the
   necessary grace in this world and everlasting
   life in the world to come,
   for this is what You have promised, and
   You always keep Your promises.

An Act of Charity

O God,
   I love you with my whole heart
   above all things,
   because You are infinitely good;
   and for Your sake
   I love my neighbor as I love myself.

The Apostles' Creed

I believe in God, the Father almighty, Creator
   of heaven and earth.
I believe in Jesus Christ, his only Son, our Lord.
   He was conceived by the power
   of the Holy Spirit
   and born of the Virgin Mary.
   He suffered under Pontius Pilate, was crucified,
   died and was buried. He descended to the dead.
   On the third day he rose again.
   He ascended into heaven,
   and is seated at the right hand
   of the Father.
   He will come again to judge

the living and the dead.
I believe in the Holy Spirit,
    the holy catholic church,
    the communion of saints,
    the forgiveness of sins,
    the resurrection of the body,
    and life everlasting.
    Amen.

The Confiteor

I confess to almighty God,
    and to you, my brothers and sisters, that I
    have sinned
    through my own fault,
    in my thoughts and in my words,
    in what I have done,
    and in what I have failed to do;
    and I ask blessed Mary, ever Virgin, all the
    angels and saints,
    and you, my brothers and sisters,
    to pray for me to the Lord our God.

Act of Contrition

My God, I am sorry for my sins
with all my heart.

In choosing to do wrong
and failing to do good,
I have sinned against You
whom I should love above all things.

I firmly intend with Your help
to sin no more, to do penance and to avoid
whatever leads me to sin. Amen.

Leonardo Da Vinci. *Saint Anne, Virgin Mary and Child Jesus,* (1452-15